Amazing life cycles

BIRDS

by Brenda Williams

An Hachette UK Company
www.hachette.co.uk

First published in the USA in 2013 by TickTock, an imprint of Octopus Publishing Group Ltd
Endeavour House, 189 Shaftesbury Avenue, London, WC2H 8JY
www.octopusbooks.co.uk www.octopusbooksusa.com

Distributed in the US by Hachette Book Group, USA, 237 Park Avenue, New York, NY 10017, USA
Distributed in Canada by Canadian Manda Group, 165 Dufferin Street, Toronto, Ontario, Canada M6K 3H6

ISBN 978 1 84898 860 6

Printed and bound in China
10 9 8 7 6 5 4 3 2 1

With thanks to Marjorie Frank
Natural history consultant: Dr. Kim Dennis-Bryan F.Z.S
US Editor: Jennifer Dixon Cover design: Steve West Production Controller: Alexandra Bell

Picture credits (t=top; b=bottom; c=center; l=left; r=right):
Corbis: 7tl, 7r, 10c, 20tl, 22c. FLPA: 6tl, 8tl, 9 main, 9tl, 15cl, 17t, 17r, 21b, 24b, 25t, 25b, 29cl, 30b.
Nature Picture Library: 26, 27. Shutterstock: OFC, 1, 2, 3, 4tl, 4–5 main, 4b, 5t, 7bl, 8c, 8b, 9tr, 10tl, 10br, 11t, 11b, 12tl, 12c, 12b, 13, 14tl, 14–15c, 14cr, 14cl, 14b, 15tl, 15tr, 15cr, 15b, 16tl, 16, 18, 19, 22tl, 23, 24tl, 28, 29r, 30tl, 31, OBC.
Superstock: 5b, 20 main, 21t. TickTock image archive: map page 6, globe page 22.

Every effort has been made to trace copyright holders, and we apologize in advance for any omissions. We would be pleased to insert the appropriate acknowledgments in any subsequent edition of this publication.

Contents

Words that look **bold like this** are in the glossary.

What is a bird?

All adult birds, including ducks, have waterproof feathers.

Birds have something that no other animals have – feathers! Other animals have wings, and other animals lay eggs, but no other animals have feathers. A bird's feathers help to keep it warm.

Flying birds have stiff feathers that help them to fly. They have small soft feathers, called "down," for keeping warm.

Millions of years ago, prehistoric **reptiles** lived on Earth. These reptiles were the **ancestors** of birds.

Birds lay eggs like reptiles, but birds are **endothermic** animals, like **mammals**.

Birds have scales on their legs and feet, and claws, like reptiles.

Birds can be tiny, like the hummingbirds in this picture, or huge, like an ostrich.

Bird habitats

This European robin has built a nest on a shelf in a garden shed!

A habitat is the place where a plant or an animal lives. Birds live in warm places, such as **rainforests**, and cold places, such as the Antarctic. Many birds live close to people, in cities or around farms.

Birds live in most of the world's habitats.

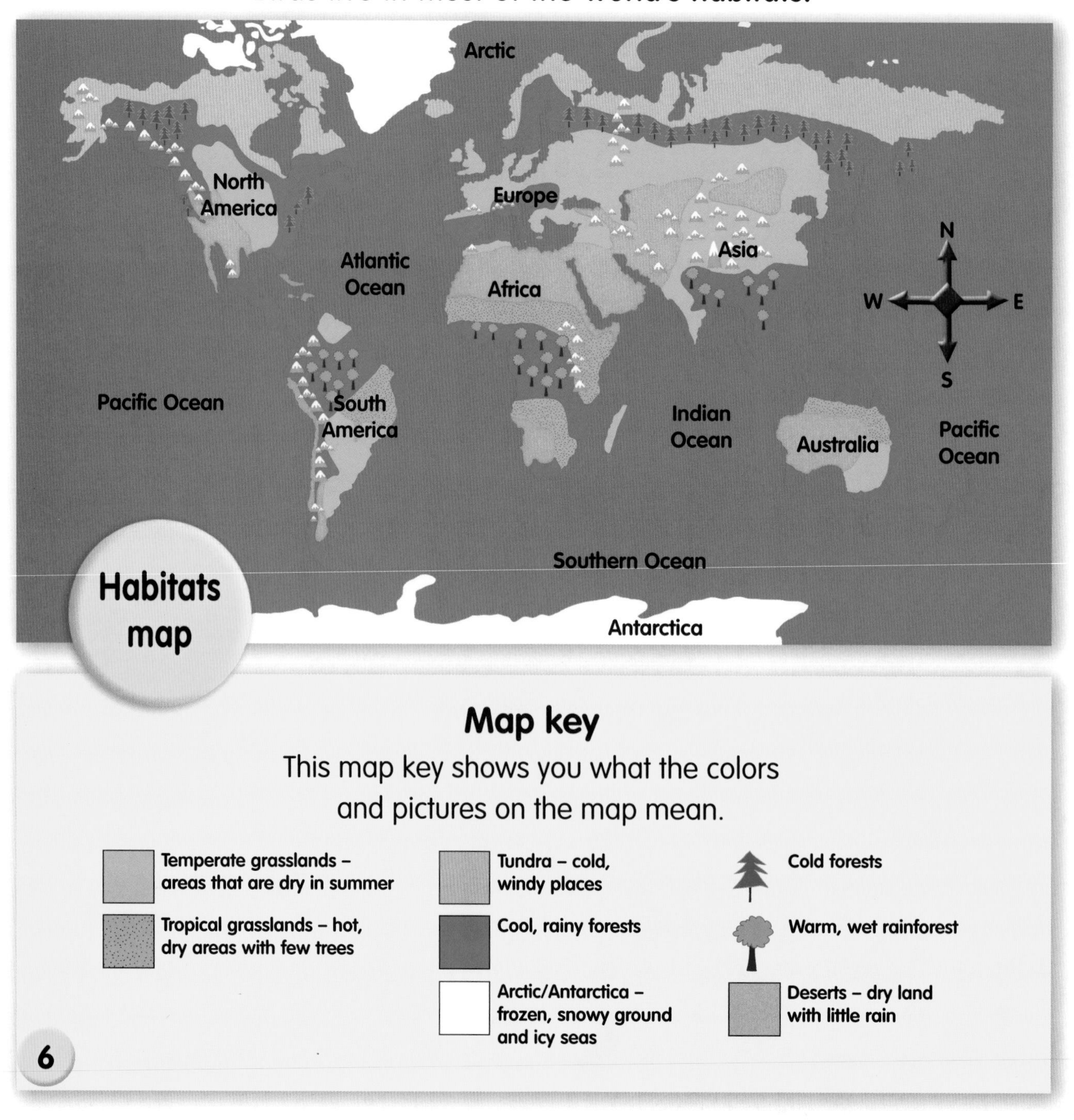

Emperor penguins breed in the Antarctic – the coldest place on Earth.

Macaws live in warm rainforests.

Emperor penguins are the biggest type of penguin.

Water-loving birds live beside rivers, lakes, or the sea. Gulls and other seabirds often build their nests on or above cliffs. They gather together in big **colonies**.

This is a gannet nesting colony near the sea.

Wings and flying

Swifts catch insects in the air.

Birds have very light bodies. Their bones are very strong. Birds have powerful muscles to beat their wings up and down. Beating their wings is hard work, and so birds spend a lot of time eating.

You can tell from a wing shape how a bird flies. A swift has long pointed wings for fast flying.

A buzzard has broad wings for gliding and soaring high in the sky.

Buzzards fly high looking out for food, such as mice, on the ground.

AMAZING BIRD FACT

A European robin's short wings are good for quick short flights from place to place, catching insects to eat.

The wandering albatross's wingspan is 11.5 feet (3.5 meters).

A pair of wandering albatrosses.

The wandering albatross has the biggest **wingspan** in the bird kingdom. It spends most of its life flying over the ocean. It flies to land when it is time to **mate**, lay eggs, and raise its young.

Baby birds flap their wings to strengthen their flight muscles before leaving the nest or the ground, like this young albatross.

Mom meets dad

A male and a female swan usually pair for life.

Most birds **breed** every year, usually in the spring. Some birds stay together as a pair for life. Other birds have a new partner each year. Some females will have chicks with more than one male in the same year.

Tail

Some male birds have colorful feathers to attract females. The male peacock shows off to the female peahen by spreading his tail feathers like a fan.

Many male birds sing to attract a female to their **territory**. They defend their territory and their female by chasing away other males.

Females are attracted to the male with the most "eyes."

Sometimes dancing is a part of the mating behavior. Female blue-footed booby birds are attracted to the males with the brightest blue feet, and the male dances to show them off.

AMAZING BIRD FACT

To attract a mate, the male frigate bird puffs out his bright red throat like a balloon.

Eggs and nests

Many female birds make a nest on their own. Others are helped by their partner. Some birds make the nest before they mate – some do it afterwards. Next, the female bird lays her eggs in the nest.

This female swan is collecting leaves to put in her nest.

Some birds make nests from grass, twigs, or leaves. The flamingo makes a nest of mud with a scooped-out top.

The white stork's nest is made of sticks. The storks add more sticks every year, and so the nest gets bigger and bigger!

The female flamingo usually lays one egg.

The female stork lays up to four eggs in her nest.

This great spotted woodpecker makes a nest in a hole in a tree.

This bald eagle is sitting on her eggs.

Female birds sit on the eggs to keep them warm. This is called **incubation**. Some males help with this job, too, and they bring food for the female.

Chicks **hatch** from the eggs. Many chicks are helpless. Often, both mom and dad bring food for the chicks.

What is a life cycle?

A life cycle is all the different **stages** and changes that a plant or animal goes through in its life. This diagram shows a bird life cycle.

A robin chick eats about 140 grubs a day!

1

An adult male and female bird meet and mate.

6

When they are ready to go off on their own, the chicks leave the nest. Some parents teach their chicks how to fly. This is a picture of a young robin.

This is the life cycle of a European robin.

5

The parents bring the chicks food to eat. Some birds remove their chicks' droppings from the nest, too!

Amazing bird life cycles

In this book we are going to find out about some amazing animal life cycles – from the record-breaking Arctic tern to the tricky killdeer.

The female lays eggs in a nest.

These robins live in Europe, North Africa, and parts of Asia.

The female sits on the eggs to keep them warm. Some male birds bring the female food while she does this.

The eggs hatch. Many chicks, including robin chicks, are blind and have no feathers when they hatch.

This is a southern ground hornbill. It feeds on the ground.

Hornbill

Hornbills live in the forests of Africa and Asia. Some hornbills use their large beak, or bill, to eat fruit, and others use it to catch insects, lizards, and frogs.

Most types of hornbills find their food in the trees, but some feed on the ground.

This great Indian hornbill lives in trees.

LIFE CYCLE FACTS
Female hornbills lay up to six eggs. The chicks hatch in about 30 to 50 days.

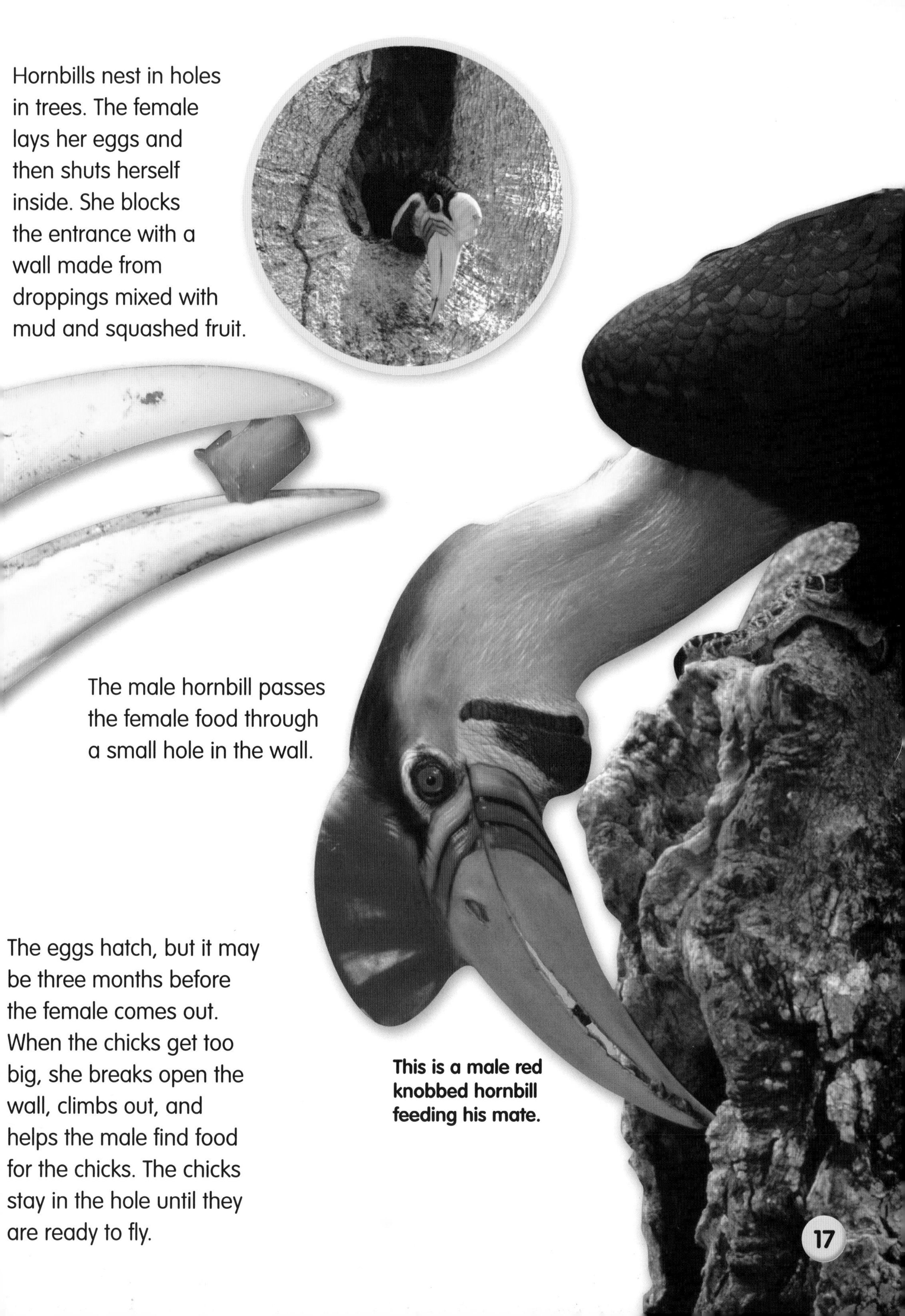

Hornbills nest in holes in trees. The female lays her eggs and then shuts herself inside. She blocks the entrance with a wall made from droppings mixed with mud and squashed fruit.

The male hornbill passes the female food through a small hole in the wall.

The eggs hatch, but it may be three months before the female comes out. When the chicks get too big, she breaks open the wall, climbs out, and helps the male find food for the chicks. The chicks stay in the hole until they are ready to fly.

This is a male red knobbed hornbill feeding his mate.

Killdeer

Killdeers live on grasslands. They eat worms, beetles, grasshoppers, and snails. Killdeers nest on the ground, where there are lots of dangers – chicks can run as soon as they hatch!

A killdeer will puff itself up, display its tail over its head, and run at a horse or cow to scare it and stop the big animal from stepping on its eggs.

The killdeer's eggs are **camouflaged** to hide them from egg-eating **predators**.

Killdeer chicks have feathers as soon as they hatch.

On the grassland there is nowhere to hide. The chicks have to sit still in the grass. Their coloration acts as camouflage

To lead predators, such as foxes, away from the nest, the killdeer has a trick. It drags one of its wings on the ground and cries out so it appears injured.

The fox follows the killdeer, thinking it will get an easy meal. The killdeer leads the fox away from the nest and then flies away. The chicks wait, keeping very still and quiet, until mom returns.

LIFE CYCLE FACTS

The female killdeer normally lays four eggs. The chicks hatch after about 24 to 28 days.

Penguin pairs stay together throughout the breeding season.

Emperor penguin

Penguins cannot fly. Their wings are modified into flippers for swimming in the sea. Emperor penguins do not build nests. After mating, the female lays one egg. The male may hold the egg on his feet or put it in a brood pouch, a patch of skin without feathers, to keep it warm.

The new chick is warm on dad's feet!

The female goes off to sea to catch fish. Sometimes emperor penguins walk for 60 miles (100 kilometers) to get to the sea.

All winter the male cares for the egg. In spring, the egg hatches, and the female returns from the sea with food for the chick.

LIFE CYCLE FACTS

The female emperor penguin lays one egg. The chick hatches after about 62 to 67 days.

Big chicks stand in a huddle to protect themselves from snow and icy winds.

When the egg has hatched, one parent takes care of the chick while the other fishes for food. When the chick can stand on the ice, both parents go fishing.

Until their adult feathers grow, the chicks cannot swim. After five or six months, the chicks' feathers grow and they are able to go to sea to find food on their own.

The parent penguin regurgitates, or brings up, partly digested fish from its throat for the chick.

Arctic tern

Arctic terns catch fish by plunging into the sea.

The Arctic tern is the champion bird traveller. Each year, this small seabird **migrates** from the Arctic to Antarctica and back again. Arctic terns fly about 25,000 miles (40,000 kilometers) around the world every year.

When it is winter in the north of the world, it is summer in the south. Arctic terns fly south to escape the cold northern winter. When the southern summer ends, they fly north again.

Arctic terns have two summers every year.

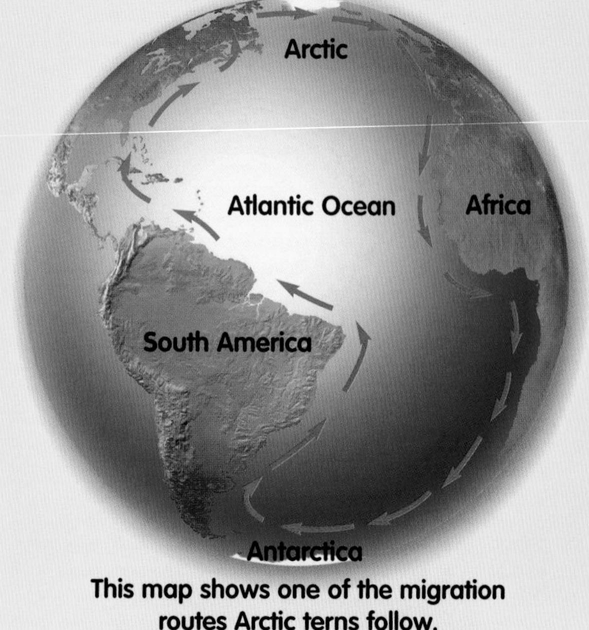

This map shows one of the migration routes Arctic terns follow.

Arctic terns pair for life. They mate and lay their eggs in the Arctic.

The parent terns raise their chicks during the short Arctic summer. When it's time to fly south, the parent terns guide the youngsters to show them the way.

LIFE CYCLE FACTS

The female Arctic tern lays one to three eggs. The chicks hatch after about 24 days.

The parents bring the chicks fish to eat.

AMAZING BIRD LIFE CYCLE

Bower bird

The satin bower bird makes an "avenue" decorated with blue and yellow objects, including berries, feathers, and manmade objects.

Bower birds live in Australia and New Guinea. The male makes a little archway, called a bower, to attract a mate. He puts colorful things such as stones, bones, feathers, or shells inside the bower. He makes a garden, too!

The male dances in and out of his bower. If the female is impressed, she may choose the male as her mate. If not, she will move on.

LIFE CYCLE FACTS

The female satin bower bird lays two or three eggs. The chicks hatch between 21 and 22 days.

Sometimes males steal decorations from each other's bowers!

This bird is taking a piece of blue Lego!

Satin bower birds like blue. A male may collect blue drinking straws, bits of blue plastic, and even ballpoint pens!

This is a pair of great bower birds.

After mating, the female bower bird makes a saucer-shaped nest for her eggs. The male stays at his bower and tries to attract another mate.

Tailorbird

Tailorbirds can be quite tame. Some nest in gardens.

The tailorbird lives in South Asia. It makes a very unusual nest! Just as a tailor sews cloth to make clothes, the tailorbird sews leaves together to make a nest.

First the tailorbird chooses a long, wide leaf. Using its beak as a needle, it sews the edges of the leaf together to make a bag shape.

For thread, the bird uses plant fibers or spider's web. It makes neat, tight stitches. Inside the leaf-bag, the bird makes a cosy nest of spider's web, bits of string – anything soft.

LIFE CYCLE FACTS
The female tailorbird lays between three and five eggs. The chicks hatch after 12 days.

This tailorbird nest has dried out. The chicks have left.

The female sits on the eggs to incubate them. Both parents feed the chicks on insects and spiders.

Puffin

Puffins eat fish – they can carry 10 small fish sideways in their beaks.

The puffin is a seabird that nests on cliffs or in burrows. Puffins are excellent swimmers. Male and female puffins do a courtship dance – they bob heads and tap beaks. Then they mate out at sea.

A courtship dance

The puffin pair digs a nest **burrow,** using their beaks and feet. Some puffins nest inside empty rabbit holes.

LIFE CYCLE FACTS

The female puffin lays one egg. The chick hatches after about 42 days.

Inside the burrow the female lays one egg. Both parents incubate the egg and catch fish for the chick when it hatches.

When the chick is six weeks old, the parents leave it. After a week on its own, the chick leaves the burrow.

The chick rushes to the sea, usually at night, when there are few predators around. Rats and seagulls will kill puffin chicks.

That's amazing!

Birds are very good parents. They care for their eggs and chicks by building them a safe, cosy home and bringing them food. But there is one bird that's a very lazy parent!

Cave swallows attach their nests to houses or cave walls, using their gummy saliva as glue.

The cuckoo lays its egg in the nest of another bird and then leaves it. The other bird may not notice the strange egg. The cuckoo chick hatches after 12 days and pushes the other eggs or chicks out of the nest.

The cuckoo gets all the food and is soon bigger than its new parents!

African weaver birds nest in colonies. Usually the male weaves a nest from grass and leaves.

An ostrich egg is the biggest egg in the bird kingdom. A hummingbird's egg is the smallest – it's about the size of a pea!

AMAZING BIRD FACT
Ostrich chicks are looked after by their dad – mom helps out.

Glossary

ancestors – The animals from which another has descended – all the earlier individuals that came before.
breed – To mate and have babies.
burrows – Tunnels or holes under the ground where some animals live.
camouflaged – Having colors, marks, or a shape that hides an animal from predators and its prey.
colonies – Large groups.
endothermic – Animals able to maintain an internal body temperature no matter how hot or cold the air or water is around them. You are endothermic!
hatch – When a baby bird or animal breaks out of its egg.
incubation – Keeping an egg warm after laying and before it hatches.
mammals – Endothermic animals with hair, which feed their babies milk.
mate – When a male and female animal meet and have babies.
migrates – Travels a long way to find food or a place to breed.
predators – Animals that hunt and kill other animals for food.
rainforests – A dense evergreen forest with over 100 inches of rainfall yearly.
regurgitates - Brings swallowed food up to the mouth.
reptiles – Animals with scales, such as snakes, lizards, and crocodiles.
stages – Different times of an animal's life when the animal changes.
territory – An area or place an animal defends and uses to feed and breed.
wingspan – The distance from the tip of one wing to the tip of the other.

Index